Stay Safe!

Road Safety

Sue Barraclough

KU-328-585

Heinemann
LIBRARY

www.heinemann.co.uk/library
Visit our website to find out more information about Heinemann Library books.

To order:
☎ Phone 44 (0) 1865 888066
📄 Send a fax to 44 (0) 1865 314091
💻 Visit the Heinemann Bookshop at www.heinemann.co.uk/library to browse our catalogue and order online.

First published in Great Britain by Heinemann Library, Halley Court, Jordan Hill, Oxford OX2 8EJ, part of Harcourt Education. Heinemann is a registered trademark of Harcourt Education Ltd.

© Harcourt Education Ltd 2008
The moral right of the proprietor has been asserted.

All rights reserved. No part of this publication may be reproduced, stored in a retrieval system, or transmitted in any form or by any means, electronic, mechanical, photocopying, recording, or otherwise, without either the prior written permission of the publishers or a licence permitting restricted copying in the United Kingdom issued by the Copyright Licensing Agency Ltd, 90 Tottenham Court Road, London W1T 4LP (www.cla.co.uk).

Editorial: Diyan Leake and Cassie Mayer
Design: Joanna Hinton-Malivoire
Illustration: Paula Knight
Picture research: Erica Martin
Production: Duncan Gilbert

Origination by Chroma Graphics (Overseas) Pte Ltd
Printed and bound in China by South China Printing Co. Ltd

ISBN 978 0 431 18436 4
12 11 10 09 08
10 9 8 7 6 5 4 3 2

British Library Cataloguing in Publication Data
Barraclough, Sue
  Road safety. - (Stay safe!)
  1. Pedestrian accidents - Prevention - Juvenile literature
  2. Traffic safety - Juvenile literature 3. Safety education
  - Juvenile literature
  I. Title
  363.1'25

Acknowledgements
The publishers would like to thank Robin Wilcox for assistance in the preparation of this book.

Every effort has been made to contact copyright holders of any material reproduced in this book. Any omissions will be rectified in subsequent printings if notice is given to the publishers.

CROYDON LIBRARIES	
3 8015 02269 544 3	
PETERS	13-Nov-2008
J363	£9.50
	BRA.CHI

Contents

Roads are busy places.

Do you know about road safety?

Never run out into a road.

Always stop at the kerb.

Never cross a road without looking and listening.

Always look both ways and listen for cars before you cross.

Never cross a road near a hill or a bend.

Always find a safe place to cross the road.

Never cross by parked cars.

Always make sure people can see you.

Never try to cross busy roads.

Always use foot bridges or subways
if you can.

Never run ahead.

Always hold hands as you cross the road.

Never play next to a road.

Always find a safe place to play.

Cross on a zebra crossing when
you can.

Always take care on the road and you will stay safe.

Road safety rules

- Stop at the kerb before crossing the road.

- Look both ways before you cross.

- Listen for cars before you cross.

- Find a safe place to cross.

- Make sure people can see you.

- Use footbridges or subways if you can.

- Hold hands as you cross the road.

- Find a safe place to play.

Picture glossary

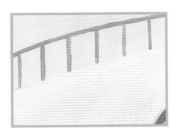 **bridge** path that goes over a road so that you can get to the other side

 **crossing** place in the road where people can cross. Crossings may have special colours or lights.

 **kerb** edge of the pavement

 **subway** path that goes under a road so that you can get to the other side

Index

Notes for parents and teachers

Before reading

Discuss road safety with the children. Talk about zebra crossings and pelican crossings. What does it mean at a crossing when the "red man" shows?

After reading

Road safety song. To the tune of "Here We Go Round the Mulberry Bush", sing the following words and do the actions: "We know how to cross the road, cross the road, cross the road, We know how to cross the road, every day of the week ... First we stand and wait at the kerb ... Then we look from right to left ... And we listen out for cars ... Then we walk across the road."

Traffic discs. Give each child a red cardboard disc and a green cardboard disc. Describe some situations near a road and ask the children to decide: road safety (hold up green disc) or road danger (hold up red disc). The situations could be things such as choosing to cross at a zebra crossing, running ahead of mum or dad, or trying to cross between parked cars.

Road safety role-play. On a roadway playmat or in the sandpit give children vehicles and play people. Encourage them to enact scenes to demonstrate road safety; for example, "The car is stopping at the zebra crossing – now it is safe to cross ... We won't cross here because there are too many parked cars ..."